I Live in the City/
Vivo en la ciudad

por Gini Holland

Reading consultant: Susan Nations, M.Ed., author/literacy coach/consultant

WEEKLY WR READER®
EARLY LEARNING LIBRARY

Please visit our web site at: **www.earlyliteracy.cc**
For a free color catalog describing Weekly Reader® Early Learning Library's
list of high-quality books, call 1-877-445-5824 (USA) or 1-800-387-3178 (Canada).
Weekly Reader® Early Learning Library's fax: (414) 336-0164.

Library of Congress Cataloging-in-Publication Data

Holland, Gini.
    (I live in the city. English & Spanish)
    I live in the city = Vivo en la ciudad / by Gini Holland.
      p. cm. — (Where I Live = Donde vivo)
    Summary: A very simple and brief description of what it is like to live in the city.
    Includes bibliographical references and index.
    ISBN 0-8368-4126-3 (lib. bdg.)
    ISBN 0-8368-4133-6 (softcover)
    1. Cities and towns—Juvenile literature. 2. City and town life—Juvenile literature.
  (1. Cities and towns. 2. City and town life. 3. Spanish language materials-Bilingual.)
  I. Title: Vivo en la ciudad. II. Title.
  HT152.H66   2004b
  307.76—dc22   2003064548

This edition first published in 2004 by
Weekly Reader® Early Learning Library
330 West Olive Street, Suite 100
Milwaukee, WI 53212 USA

Copyright © 2004 by Weekly Reader® Early Learning Library

Editor: JoAnn Early Macken
Art direction and page layout: Tammy West
Picture research: Diane Laska-Swanke
Photographer: Gregg Andersen

Printed in the United States of America

4 5 6 7 8 9 10 09 08 07 06

Note to Educators and Parents

Reading is such an exciting adventure for young children! They are beginning to integrate their oral language skills with written language. To encourage children along the path to early literacy, books must be colorful, engaging, and interesting; they should invite the young reader to explore both the print and the pictures.

Where I Live is a new series designed to help children read about everyday life in other places. In each book, young readers will learn interesting facts about different locations from the viewpoints of children who live there.

Each book is specially designed to support the young reader in the reading process. The familiar topics are appealing to young children and invite them to read — and re-read — again and again. The full-color photographs and enhanced text further support the student during the reading process.

In addition to serving as wonderful picture books in schools, libraries, homes, and other places where children learn to love reading, these books are specifically intended to be read within an instructional guided reading group. This small group setting allows beginning readers to work with a fluent adult model as they make meaning from the text. After children develop fluency with the text and content, the book can be read independently. Children and adults alike will find these books supportive, engaging, and fun!

— Susan Nations, M.Ed., author, literacy coach, and consultant in literacy development

I live in the city.

Vivo en la ciudad.

Cars and trucks
drive by.

— — — — — — —

Los carros y
camiones pasan
y pasan.

I shop in big stores
in the city.

Voy de compras
a almacenes
grandes en la
ciudad.

9

Bright lights shine
in the city.

Las luces de la
ciudad brillan.

Police sirens are loud in the city.

- - - - - - -

Las sirenas de la policía hacen ruido en la ciudad.

Ice cream trucks play songs.

- - - - - - -

Los camiones que venden helado tienen música.

Brendon's
ICE CREAM EXPRESS

FOR SPECIAL
OCCASIONS
Call 307-333-8981

MOBILE
CATERING
SERVICE

K2

SAFE
FIRST
CROSS
REAR

15

I play in the
city park.

- - - - - -

Juego en el
parque.

I visit the city museum.

Visito el museo.

I like to live in
the city.

- - - - - - -

Me gusta vivir
en la ciudad.

Glossary

museum — a place where people can see interesting things
museo — lugar donde se pueden ver cosas interesantes

park — land set aside for play and gardens
parque — lugar que se destina para juegos y jardines

shop — to look for something to buy
hacer compras — buscar cosas para comprar

sirens — warning sounds made by emergency vehicles and police cars
sirenas — sonidos de aviso de vehículos de emergencia y de la policía

For More Information

Books/Libros

Daniels, Patricia, ed. *Do Skyscrapers Touch the Sky? First Questions and Answers about the City*. Alexandria, Virginia: Time-Life for Children, 1994.

Milich, Zoran. *The City ABC Book*. Toronto: Kids Can Press, 2001.

Sayre, April Pulley. *It's My City!* A Singing Map. New York: Greenwillow, 2001.

Sonpiet, Chris K. *Around Town*. New York: Lothrop, Lee, and Shepard Books, 1994.

Web Sites/Páginas Web

City Creator

www.citycreator.com/
Drag and drop roads, buildings, vehicles, and people to create your own city

Index

About the Author

Gini Holland is a writer and an editor. The author of over twenty nonfiction books for children, she was also a long-time educator for Milwaukee Public Schools, both in the elementary classroom and as a staff development instructor for both special education and general education teachers. She lives with her husband in Milwaukee, Wisconsin, and is a devoted fan of their son's two Chicago-based bands.